POPULAR PET CARE

Hamsters and Gerbils

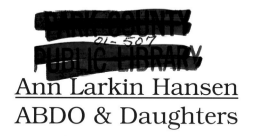

 <u>Ann Larkin Hansen</u>
ABDO & Daughters

Pets are more than just toys or play things. They are part of our families. It is important to love and care for them. Popular Pet Care will help you understand your pet and know of its unique needs. Remember that your pet will depend on you to be responsible in caring for it.

Dr. David C. Hallstrom—Veterinarian

Published by Abdo & Daughters, 4940 Viking Drive, Suite 622, Edina, Minnesota 55435.

Copyright © 1997 by Abdo Consulting Group, Inc., Pentagon Tower, P.O. Box 36036, Minneapolis, Minnesota 55435 USA. International copyrights reserved in all countries. No part of this book may be reproduced in any form without written permission from the publisher.

Printed in the United States.

Cover Photo credits: Vik Orenstein
Interior Photo credits: Vik Orenstein, Peter Arnold, Inc., Animals Animals, Superstock, Connie Bickman
Illustrations and Icons by: C. Spencer Morris

Edited by Julie Berg
Contributing editor Dr. David C. Hallstrom—Veterinarian
Special thanks to our Popular Pet Care kids:
Peter Dumdei, Gracie Hansen, Brandon Isakson, Laura Jones, Annie O'Leary, Peter Rengstorf, Morgan Roberts, and Tyler Wagner

Library of Congress Cataloging-in-Publication Data

Hansen, Ann Larkin.
    Hamsters and gerbils / Ann Larkin Hansen.
    p. cm. -- (Popular pet care)
    Includes index.
    Summary: Describes the housing, feeding, care, and handling of hamsters and gerbils.
    ISBN 1-56239-783-4
    1. Hamsters as pets--Juvenile literature. 2. Gerbils as pets--Juvenile literature. [1. Hamsters. 2. Gerbils. 3. Pets.] I. Title II. Series: Hansen, AnnLarkin. Popular Pet care.
    SF459.H3H27   1997
    636.9'356--dc21   97-5703
                                         CIP
                                         AC

Contents

Small Furry Creatures 4

Hamsters.. 6

Gerbils 8

Cages 10

Food And Water 12

Health 14

Handling 16

Playing With Your Pet 18

Accidents and Escapes 20

Choosing Which Pet... 22

When Hamsters and Gerbils Die 24

Glossary 28

Index 31

Small Furry Creatures

Would you like a pet you can hold in your hand? One that is furry and warm and fun to play with? A gerbil or hamster is a wonderful pet for a kid. They are quiet and take up hardly any space. They are easy to care for and can be left alone for a few days if you go on a short trip.

These animals are **rodents**, just like mice, guinea pigs, rabbits, beaver, and squirrels. Rodents have teeth that are always growing, so they need to chew to keep their teeth short. Make sure your pet always has cardboard, hard wood (not pine), or other **chew toys**.

Hamster

Gerbil

Hamsters

Hamsters come from the desert, where they live underground in long **burrows**. They have pouches in their cheeks for storing food, and they don't drink much water. They have short, stumpy tails.

Hamsters come in many different colors, and some have long hair. Get a short-haired hamster unless you have time every day for brushing.

Buy just one hamster. Two hamsters in a cage will nearly always fight. But hamsters do become very tame if they are handled often in a gentle way. They also like **exercise wheels** in their cages. Hamsters live for about three years.

A hamster on an exercise wheel.

Gerbils

Gerbils also come from the desert, but they have long tails and no cheek pouches. Where a hamster will climb, a gerbil will jump. Gerbils like to bury their food and thump their feet when they are alarmed. They are more active but harder to tame than hamsters. Gerbils usually live for four or five years.

Gerbils like company. It's best to buy two females from the same **litter**, since males might fight when they grow older. Usually gerbils are brown, but sometimes other colors are available. Gerbils can break their tails in an **exercise wheel**. Instead, give them plenty of cardboard boxes and tubes to play in and chew.

Pick up a gerbil by the base of its tail, right next to the body. Never pick up a gerbil by the end of the tail.

Gerbils have long tails and no cheek pouches.

Cages

A ten gallon **aquarium** with a screen lid is the best cage for gerbils and hamsters. It lasts the longest and is easy to clean. Or you can buy a **modular** plastic cage, putting the parts together like a maze for your pet. Every cage needs a **water bottle** that hangs on the side, and a heavy food dish that can't be tipped over.

Use cedar chips or ripped newspaper for **bedding**. Do not use kitty litter, but a little grass and leaves is okay. Tear the newspaper the long way into one inch wide strips, and use a lot. Once each week, take out all the old stuff, wipe down the cage with a damp rag, and put in fresh bedding.

An aquarium with a lid.

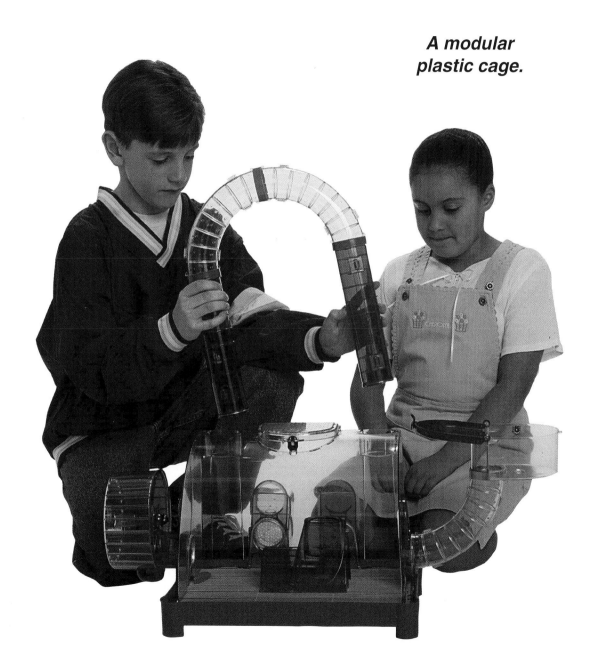

A modular plastic cage.

Food And Water

Keep the **water bottle** full, and make sure the tube at the bottom doesn't touch any of the **bedding**. If it does, the water will all drain out and you'll have a soggy mess. Once a week, use an old toothbrush to scrub out the inside of the bottle to keep algae from growing.

Buy food for your pet at the grocery store or pet store. Put a little in every day, or just fill the dish every few days. Don't worry if it gets buried or hidden by your pet. Once a week, throw out the old food.

For treats, your pet might like most fruits, vegetables, cheese, or bread. But don't feed it raw beans, cabbage, or raw potatoes, since these might make your pet ill. Grass and weeds that haven't been sprayed are a very good treat.

*A hamster sitting on its bedding. Vegetables are
a favorite treat for your pet.*

13

Health

Buy an animal that is quite young, usually just a few weeks old. Make sure the eyes are shiny, and the fur around them is clean and dry. All the fur should look thick and healthy, and there should not be any sores or bare spots on the body.

Gerbils and hamsters are healthy animals. If they have a clean cage, and fresh food and water, they shouldn't get sick. Don't put the cage in the hot sun or a cold **draft**. A quiet corner is best.

If your pet has runny eyes, bare spots, sniffles, or has been injured, call a **veterinarian**. Usually the only treatment is to leave it quietly in its cage. Be careful when handling your pet, since most are injured by falling out of their owner's hands.

Gerbils need fresh food and water to stay healthy.

Handling

Handle your pet gently every day, and it will become tame. Never squeeze your pet, and don't make sudden movements or loud noises. Never grab it by the leg or the end of the tail. Pets that are handled roughly will bite. Hamsters are usually tamer and less jumpy than gerbils.

After you bring your new pet home, give it a day or two to get used to its new house. Then introduce yourself by laying your hand on the bottom of the cage. Your pet will learn to climb all over your hand. After a couple days you can gently pick it up, holding it with both hands so it can't jump.

Opposite page: Always handle your pet with care.

Playing With Your Pet

To play with your pet outside its cage, first get the room ready. Close the door and unplug everything. Pull the furniture out a little so you can reach behind it.

Now you can turn your pet loose. It may explore the room, or it may explore you as you sit on the floor! Don't put your pet up on furniture where it might fall and break a leg or tail. Be sure to clean up any messes it makes, and make sure it doesn't chew any wires.

Never take your hamster or gerbil outside. A sudden noise or movement might cause them to jump and run, and you may never see your pet again.

Playing with your pet is fun.

Accidents and Escapes

If your gerbil or hamster escapes, close all the doors to the area you know it is in. Put some food in a small, deep box, and stand it in the middle of the room. Use a piece of cardboard or a long wood block to make a ramp from the floor to the open top of the box. Sooner or later your pet will get hungry, smell the food, run up the ramp, and jump into the box to eat.

If you can't wait a few days for this trick to work, you will need two or three people. One person should be ready to pop a bucket or box over your pet after the others scare it gently out into the open.

It's better to stop escapes before they happen. Make sure you have a firm hold on your gerbil's tail or

your hamster's back while carrying it around. The
lid to the cage should fit tightly, since gerbils will
sometimes jump and knock the lid open.

*Always keep a
good watch on
your pet.*

Choosing Which Pet

Deciding whether to get a gerbil or a hamster may be hard. Go to the pet store, and watch for a while. The hamsters are chubby and gentle. The gerbils are quick and curious. Pick the one you enjoy the most. The salesperson at the pet store will help you pick out a pet, a cage, food dish, **water bottle**, and the right food. Keep your new pet warm and quiet until you get it home.

Once you choose, treat your new pet gently and kindly. Keep the cage clean, and the food and water fresh. Give your pet lots of things to chew up, but never cloth or cotton. Your pet will be happy and healthy, and you will enjoy the company!

Opposite page: Always keep your pet's cage clean.

When Hamsters and Gerbils Die

Hamsters and gerbils usually live for three to five years. As they get old they may slow down a little, though usually nothing seems to change at all. But one morning, you will get up to find that your pet has died peacefully in its sleep. It's okay to feel sad about losing a pet. You can also feel proud of yourself if your pet had a good life, with fresh water, a clean cage, and gentle handling. You did everything you could do.

You can bury the body in a spot away from buildings and places where people walk or play. Or it might be easiest to just wrap it in a plastic bag and put it in the garbage. Your pet won't mind.

Clean and disinfect the cage and equipment. You may have a friend or relative that would like to have it, or you may be ready for another pet!

Hamsters and gerbils make good pets.

Glossary

Aquarium: A glass tank, usually for keeping fish, but also used for other small animals.

Bedding: A layer of soft material for your pet to dig in, chew up, go to the bathroom on, and hide in. Cedar chips and ripped newspaper are the most common bedding, but you could also try hay, straw, or even sand. Kitty litter is not a good bedding material.

Burrow: An underground chamber that an animal will dig for a home, sometimes with a long tunnel.

Chew Toys: Anything your pet chews on to keep its teeth short. Cardboard and hardwood sticks are good, and many pet stores have chew toys for sale. Do not use pine or other soft woods, or plastic.

Draft: Air movement inside the house, like a very light breeze. Pets kept in a draft will often get colds.

Exercise Wheel: A wheel on a frame. The pet gets inside the wheel and runs, turning it around and round. Gerbils do learn to use exercise wheels safely, but you must watch them closely for a while.

Litter: A group of brothers and sisters. Gerbils and hamsters have several babies at once, and this is called the litter.

Modular: Something that comes in different pieces that all fit any other piece. Modular cages can be a lot of fun for both the pet and the owner, and you can keep adding to them.

Rodents: A family of mammals distinguished by teeth that are continuously growing. All rodents need to chew or gnaw constantly to keep their teeth from becoming too long for their mouths.

Veterinarian: An animal doctor.

Water Bottle: A plastic or glass bottle with a lid containing a bent, metal tube. Filled with water and hung upside down in the cage with a metal holder, the bottle allows your pet to drink without spilling or getting the water dirty with bedding.

Index

A

algae 12
aquarium 10

B

beans 12
beaver 4
bedding 10, 12
bread 12
brush 6, 12
burrow 6

C

cage 6, 10, 14, 16, 18, 21, 22, 24
cheeks 6, 8
cheese 12
chew toy 4
color 6, 8

D

desert 6, 8
draft 14

E

escape 20
exercise wheel 6, 8
eyes 14

F

feet 8
female 8
fight 6, 8
food 6, 8, 10, 12, 14, 20, 22
fruits 12
fur 4, 14

G

grass 10, 12
guinea pig 4

H

hair 6
handling 6, 14, 24
health 14, 22
home 16, 22

J

jump 8, 16, 18, 20, 21

L

leaves 10
litter 8, 10, 28

M

male 8
mice 4
modular cage 10

P

pet 4, 10, 12, 14, 16, 18, 20, 22
potatoes 12

R

rabbit 4
rodent 4

S

squirrel 4

T

tail 6, 8, 16, 18, 20
tame 6, 8, 16
teeth 4

V

vegetables 12
veterinarian 14

W

water 6, 10, 12, 14, 22
water bottle 10, 12, 22